CREEP LOVE

MICHAEL WALSH

Autumn House Press receives state arts funding support through a grant from the Pennsylvania Council on the Arts, a state agency funded by the Commonwealth of Pennsylvania, and the National Endowment for the Arts, a federal agency.

Cover design: Melissa Dias-Mandoly

ISBN: 9781938769764
LCCN: 2020947434

TABLE OF CONTENTS

I.

II.

III.

IV.

V.

VI.

VII.

I.

TO THE BRIGHTNESS

Other survivors
of near-death experiences have found joy
when they think of how they winked off
then on like fireflies,
how they flew the warm, safe
descent to their waiting chests.
But my half-death was dirty.
My brain burned into itself
a scar, palm and eye
cross-wired into a witch:
hand as hallucination
or secret mouth.
Know, by now, I have mastered
my eyeless familiar,
fetch of the lost,
its wisdom opposite
all brightness: fuck your pity.
Be happily nobody.

FENCE CATCHING HEART

Wanting out no matter what, the cow jumped.
Standing on watch along the fence line,
suddenly in the path of her leap, I fell
to the ground to dodge her havoc of hooves.
Landing clear, she pulled the four live wires
loose from the posts down onto me,
their pulse taking over mine.
She entangled me in her need to get free.
My parents watched, unmoving, amused.
With each shock, my limbs blinked
into disconnection. To get free fast,
these hands had to lift, these legs had to kick
the wires. They snapped back into place
like puppet strings. Eyes going black
in the aftershocks
had to be shut. Then this body
had to turn off and twist loose.
After the first few attempts,
I thought they would run to the switch,
cut my voltage, grab my shoulders, pull.

FAMILY SOCIAL SERVICES

We were sent to three different therapists,
their task to keep the family together
for Christ. My stepdad, sister, and me
get cross-examined. Mine asks
if my stepdad's ever done things I don't talk about.
It's risky, but I take this one chance,
say everything so far. My guy writes it all down.
The next session, I learn my guy has shared my stories
with my stepdad's guy, who has shared my stories
with my stepdad, and they talked about the things
I say he's done. Now he knows.
I thought they would pull me from the home,
but I go back into the creep's care.
At least now I know everything we say
will get written down, passed around, changed
first in the session notes, then in the conversation
with the next patient, and later in between
these good men in their sanctimonious next steps.

At dinner, on the days after my stepdad has received talk therapy
for intermittent explosive disorder—
that do-nothing excuse he uses for bad behavior—I sometimes catch
his pissed-off, silent look, wonder how
our triangulated humiliation—his role as biggest brat—
really feels. If I look too long, he'll decide
to act according to his junk diagnosis,
its helpless reflex of rage.
He'll throw his milk into my sister's eyes,
and when I say *leave her alone, you fuckwad,*
he'll throw the empty at my plate,
white slivers bursting from a mine, thudding
against the shield of my glasses.
Yes, I'll tell my therapist, who will retell
the truth of the tale recorded, checked
and rechecked against the other clients.

THE GHOST STORY THEY TELL ABOUT ME

I never know when I'm shaking her, making her
wake up to listen to whoever's speaking
with my mouth: *those fools*

asleep in the farmhouse, the lights
starting to bleed. The bulbs fill like IV bags.
Zombie deputies are knocking

on the cellar door in search of new freezers
for head-meats. I won't go
back to bed. *Mom and Dad*

have been buried alive with feeding tubes
underneath the field. A man's glowing.
He drives farm to farm, sprays soup

through a hose from the steel tank
strapped to his back. Everybody's gotta eat.
I start counting out loud

the number of traps set for werewolves
who can't turn human, the headstones the family
removes, replaces with Styrofoam fakes.

THE QUEER AS ELECTRON

Knowing my identity
        in the family could shift
    with each observer, I watched

        how a turn of phrase, a silence could switch me
from brother to cousin, from momma's boy
        to daddy's bad seed, from gay

    to confused virgin, and back again
        in the blink of a sentence.
    Without moving, I dodged them.

    Inside the whirling cloud,
I formed myself in opposition
        to their background radiation.

MONK OF THE NEGATIVE

Clutching your throat, his hand
lifts your teenage body

to the barn wall. His body
presses into you, face

an inch away, eyes entering
your pupils, spare hand

adding more force now.
The ring his ten fingers form

mirrors the dark rings
you're beginning to see

around the edge of each eye.
You understand what his hands

have wanted, have found
the permission to say. You fight

his face, pull its hair, punch
its eye. Both of yours

going out, you evaporate
somewhere deeper

than soul or brain.
Not a fall to anywhere

but the obliteration of every atom,
accompanied by an oscillation

between bodiless peace
and black-hole fear.

You stay still; you spin
at the same time. For a day,

then a week, many weeks,
then months. Until he throws

the body you don't sense or know.
Your cheek scraped against

the floor returns, the rest of you
numb from neck to toe,

back to your weight
which must stand and say

I'm fine. Now wherever you go,
your body moves parallel

to the double who meditates
motionless inside you. Your hand

against the wall senses
it's endless inside, understands the stone

you clutch and squeeze
contains only the emptiness,

a calming burst of antimatter
your pressure releases.

II.

MY MOTHER AS A PREGNANT TEENAGE RUNAWAY

In Denver, she's going to give me up.
Right now, she's walking along a highway
in Montana, far from everyone who will make her
keep me, a senior-year mistake
with an ex-con who's already hustling
her look-alike little sister. Walking in the sun,
she eats only my vitamins
like war rations.

Homeless now, she sleeps in a shelter,
wondering whether I'm girl or boy, making lists
of my names, good, respectable ones,
until one day, she's walking to a pay phone
to call her grandma, says she can't,
she's coming home, please forgive her.

I want her to hand me over to that childless couple,
forget about me, change her name, keep hitchhiking
to San Francisco, Portland, anywhere but back
to what's waiting: the steel pipe he keeps
in the barn beams, my father knocking up
my aunt with two boys, the family shame
of being the slut who slept with him first.
I want her to ditch me, but she won't.
She calls home, no one knowing if she's even alive,
locks her cast-off life to mine.

SCRATCHED-OUT NAME

In my aunt's house, at least my father got to hang,
the absent dad in a picture frame. Within minutes
        on my first visit, she handed me his photo,

a generosity, a face I'd never seen. He looked
so proper, buttoned-up and trimmed
        to a normal pop, not the nutjob

who preyed on my mother and aunt,
propositioned their little sisters too,
        his daisy chain of perversion

incomplete until he tried each one.
Were there other girls? Was this story even real?
        My aunt said she'd asked his family all kinds of questions

for years and only gotten the runaround—
everyone related to him was so tricky.
        I swallowed all my questions like sins.

IN THE DREAM MISTAKEN FOR A MEMORY

You wait for my teenage aunt in your sports car in the alley
behind my grandparents' house. They say you never dared

approach so close. Everyone but my grandparents knows
my aunt is hurrying with her eyeliner because her true love's

here early. Yes, it's wrong. Maybe I'm not your son. Maybe
my mother made it all up. I'm sitting underneath

the kitchen table, my back against the wall
where it should be obvious to anyone you're idling,

impatient for a piece. No one knows I'm hiding here,
like no one but my aunt is supposed to know

you're out there, the cyclops eye of your cigarette huffing red.
I've already looked. You didn't spot me. I want you

to take a risk, you chicken, and show yourself. Walk up here
and knock on the back door, let yourself in

so everyone knows. I wait and wait the way you're waiting
for her to finish her schoolgirl's face in the mirror.

SLEEPWALKS

In search of sleep detectors,
he pounds a hammer into walls,
waking everyone else.

~

One morning on her desk: a letter
her own hand wrote in the German
she can't remember how to read.

~

He wakes curled inside the dirt hole
his dogs dug as their bed.
Sniffing his hair, they growl.

~

Every night, more preposterous claims.
Rats scratch inside their wedding rings,
zombies blog their children's growth spurts.

~

Wild bees, she whispers,
ear to the motel wall,
tongue buzzing against teeth.

~

With a sigh of relief, he pees
into the rows of shoes of all his relatives
staying overnight for the holiday.

~

Her camera full of pictures. The same
corner of one room. At night, she watches
the fossil of a ghost float there.

~

In tighty-whities, he paces
aisles of the corner store, billfold
in hand. The clerk rings up another raincoat.

III.

DICK

My father's first name was the rutting truth.
We were all supposed to forget, but how?

Also known as the tale of Tricky Dick,
his story lived with the family

like a dirty limerick. Unaware
in my tighty-whities at twelve,

I hadn't known it had grown.
It caught my parents' eyes,

drawn down before I realized
whose chub that might be

between my legs, the only part
belonging to his bastard. I didn't

want it. What if he treated women like dogs
because he sucked cock in secret?

What if wishing for contact with the man
had turned me gay? What if

wanting none did? I didn't
want to relive his life. The family

imagined my life as a priest.
Only God could have the power.

PASTORAL, UNDERFOOT

In steel-toed boots, my sister's father was as mean
    as a machine gun. Once, fences down
        but full of current, the cows
    chowing flowers, she and her dad, my mother and I
gave chase. The wild heifers ran free,
        fearful of us. Far across the field, I saw
    my nine-year-old sister step on a wire, collapse
        to the grass, start to cry. Loathing the echo
of his own pain within her sob, her father started stomping on her
    the way he once squished a pregnant mouse
        in the oats, fetuses bursting
    pink from its side. Facedown,
all three hundred pounds of him
        brought to bear through that boot
    against her spine—she was supposed to shut up. She couldn't.
            Thirteen, I ran toward her shouting his first name,
his full name, getting closer and louder
    the way a father handles a son
        who won't listen, commanding him to *stop*,
stop that right now, until the words
inverted us, his gaze furious against the authority in mine.
        He froze. I was going to take
    his daughter, bruised to the bone.
        Was he going to defend his claim,
charge at me? I wasn't ready to be a father. I was ready
    to run faster than his fat ass
        could catch—my daughter, his daughter,
    safe in hand—get to the road,
wave down anybody, show them
        her back, his boot prints blooming purple,
    winding around her vertebrae. Instead,
        like a teenage bad boy
in a fender bender, he fled the scene.

THE COUSIN ACT

My mom says my baby cousin is really my brother.
        I'm eight, toothbrush in hand in front of the mirror
in which that startled boy inspects himself,

        not yet understanding what they've done. They don't
want me to know, but my mom doesn't believe
        in keeping secrets. That's why she's telling me,

all of a sudden, right here. There's more. The toothpaste
        spit like grief and splattered on the sink turns whiter.
My aunt's pregnant with a son by my father again.

        I know he calls from time to time, threatens
to kill my mother and me. To tell or not tell the truth
        is my aunt's choice, but in the meantime,

my mother's in trouble for telling me.
        No one else thinks I should know. I can't
say anything when we visit. Out of respect

        for my aunt, she quietly makes me keep this pact.
Thus, the family's silences begin: who really loved who
        and who didn't, how long it went on under whose nose,

how my aunt could have the sons of a man
        who put my mother through hell; what happened between
my mother, aunt, and father in any combination;

        who needs to forget about it, give it to God,
stop asking. Against my mother's protests,
        the good women decide I'm young enough

to be changed. They train me to play the cousin,
        say it. Their disappointment, otherwise, the embarrassment—
I learn what's more important.

THE LUCKIEST

When I think of the older sister I barely know, her mother
I've never met, the days when my father was on the lam
    after lighting their house on fire—the climax
of beating his high school sweetheart and the shots he took at her
inside their house—I most remember the story of the bullet
    going through the wall two inches over my sister's head
in the crib. Through that hole I hear the rants
of his drunken, teenage ghost, his presence
    gathering force like a gas leak, source and spark.
The two went into hiding and the family men
stocked up on guns, fortified the farm and waited
    for my father, certain of an attack
in the night that never came. I think he preferred the terror
of the threat to any firearm or fist.
    Though she says I'm luckiest for never meeting him,
I think she's the luckier one—the firstborn girl
whose family, like a shield wall, surrounded her.

SHUT

In their den within straw, the kittens crawl.
    When the mother goes hunting, their sealed eyes
strain against lids, follow the daylight
    seeping into bales, the yellow doubling.

From crevices they emerge, white with orange
    lightning down the tail, black
with white paws. Soft in the palm, they don't know
    where they've been, where they are,

where the boots and hooves will stomp
    like minotaurs. I stuff them
back inside their prickly passages,
    crawlspaces winding beyond reach.

I had no idea what I was learning
    when I read *Helter Skelter*, met The Family,
observed the reconstructed murder of Sharon Tate,
    complete with black-and-white crime scene photos,
and took into my mind the confession of Susan Atkins:
    how she wanted to cut out Tate's unborn baby
but didn't have the time. In these pages, I suspected my mother
    had discovered a truth regarding her and her sister's
dates with my father. One time she told me,
    Mind control was involved. A man could convince a woman
to want to slice open a pregnant girl,
    remove the child for fun. I wondered
if my father was working on our brains
    right now, according to a program that ran
without his presence. When I read about
    the Zodiac Killer, I started to think about the perp
still out there in California or Nevada, identity
    and whereabouts unknown, my father believed to be
somewhere in between Colorado, Minnesota, and Florida,
    and in the light of these scare stories,
capable of anything. Was his controlled absence
    part of his head fake? I imagined my mother
turning each page of this pulp and thinking,
    I'm not going to become her. I turned each page
wondering why they never say what happens to the maniac's son.

TO THE SPECTER

Everyone's story is wrong.
    I might know nothing
but this craze they released

inside my DNA. My brother says
    I'm the son most like you. I've tried
two last names, neither yours, none fitting.

I've studied Wieners and Roethke for the glare
    of your asylum, watched my hands
like two murderers for warning tics,

twitches. Without any
    firsthand memory of your skin
or the smell of your smoke, I'm the glue

attracting your ghost. But I don't
    bear you forward. Your opposite,
not an X-ray. I'm shaking you loose.

IV.

THE LIKELY DARKNESS

The day of the strangulation, I went to the green phone
in the barn, wrapped its curling, twisted cord
around my wrist, picked up the receiver, and rested
my pointer finger on its zero. But I couldn't imagine
rescue. More likely, shrink talk: *You say*
you were strangled? And you feel like you died
and a whole different person has, as you say,
come back? Who is this person? And the part
about surfaces. When you touch a door,
nothingness emerges from within it?
Would you say you aren't really here?
The darkness of that future
was what I could see: asylum time
with my father, the attack, the lie,
my stepdad saying, *I never.*

On the first and second days,
my body still vibrated from the zap
of my return. Someone new started
settling into the muscles, the heavy
collection of bones wanting to drag.

Each day for three days, the winding bruises
darkened, his fingerprints even more clear
to people at the lakeshore, the farm
next door, the line at the grocery store
and gas station, the animal barns at the fair.
Look away quickly—the lesson.

Each time I touched a door or wall,
darkness rolled like a wave
where palm met surface,
blinded the mind for a moment,
and rippled queasy through the body.
That dark, I knew. My mother said
I'd been unconscious for a minute,

but I'd been gone for months.
I commanded my hands to stop
bringing me back there.

By the fourth day, the bruises were fading. By the fifth,
someone could've said, wrestling rug burn.
By the sixth, hickey, and by the seventh, rash.

Each day until they were gone, I made myself walk
from the mirror in the bathroom
to the zero on the green phone,
where I hung my finger like a traitor,
snaked the comfort of the cord
around one arm, phone in hand, and considered
who to call. Closing my eyes,
floating again, I chose no one.

SUMMER INTRUDER

First tools go missing in explanations of little kids
moving stuff. Then it's license plates unscrewed
from our cars and trucks, gone, a *whodunit*.
A week later, the cows are all out of the barn,
deep in alfalfa. Partial heel and zigzag
treads turn up in mud. *Two people?*
Only one? Cops don't know. *Do you have enemies?*
Anyone making threats? In the middle of the night,
my stepdad goes outside with his shotgun,
fires five times straight-up.
Someone's scared now, in the boxelders
behind the house. Someone crashing
through branches drops a flashlight, gives no clue.

SEX WITH JESUS

Swarthy and long-haired, he was the kink
     of my wet dreams. Too young
to know if I was top, bottom, or what. But after

the first time, I knew I'd never become the priest
     my family wanted without the full confession:
how bad boy Jesus, deep inside me,

put my hands on his halo, told me to work it down
     around his neck, tight until he came. Afterwards
he detached, fastened it to my throat, choked me wet.

It never hurt. As I slept, my neck could feel
     his warm, soothing glow. Becoming
a man of the cloth, I could redeem

everyone in my family, offer forgiveness
     as a matter of my nature, explain away my lack
of desire for girls, which I'd still have to hide,

but I chose my Jesus instead.
     He'd keep returning like a golden incubus
who slipped my fist into his ass, sat on my face

until I loved rimming, and in a feat
     of prowess, fucked and sucked me,
blasphemous rapture I'll never believe was sin.

THE ANTIGAY RETELLING OF MY LIFE

Some bad gene from your psycho father
switched on or off, who knows

what's inside you. Maybe you really worry,
if you got a nice wife, had a son,

he'd become the next Dahmer?
What mother would've kept and loved

a creep's queer. She turned your willy
crooked in the womb, thank

the Lord, turned you off every girl except her.
Did your mother try to have sex with you? Did you ever

try it with a girl even once? Little boys
do get stuck on their buttholes.

Every pervert you blow is a cry for your daddy.
Your mother should've raised you right

in the church, prayed away the crazy and the gay.
Without God, you ended up a junkie,

hooked on the high of a man,
his dick the dirty needle.

GRANARY ZEN

After dark, screwed-up days,
I sit in the oats like a pile of sand,

scoop warm kernels and pour
their power onto my head,

one handful after another.
I let their dryness shrivel

my whole being. In my throat,
the scream stops being wet.

ANTICIPATION OF THE KNIFE

The dyke couple at the conference thinks I should consider pain
as medicine. They explain their histories of physical and sexual abuse

at the hands of their fathers, how ropes, clamps, and knives
help them take control. When the leather guy I'm dating

mentions he's trained in scarification
and offers to cut me, I don't say no. It's queer zen.

I've never considered the power of controlling the hurt
someone gives me. I ask to see the knife sometime.

He carries it with him. He's French and very handsome.
I wonder to whom I'm talking. I believe he would start

when I want, stop with my safe word. The pain's
not the problem, just my darker sense

that clamps and knives can't reach the nerves
dangling disconnected, lanterns deep inside.

V.

SWITCH OR AXE

Because someone has to go back, I return
to that boy showering, unaware of his stepdad
listening at the bathroom door with its little hook
for a lock. The man decides he's had it
with the wife's kid: it's time to get a stick.
Get out now, I tell the boy, *get dressed,*
grab your smokes, a change of clothes,
the phone number of someone you love
who's not related, and run. Whether he can hear
right then doesn't matter. One day
he'll understand who he had to save.

Leaving the kid, I follow my stepdad with the plan
outside to the spring trees bending green.
I tell the man, dead fifteen years now,
I found a way to forgive,
but stop anyway. Don't transmit
your childhood—the axe through the TV
when you were watching Saturday morning cartoons,
and when you cried, the fists to your face.

One day his heart will break
over what he's about to do. But today
he twists the green meat of a thick branch
until it snaps, strips the fresh bark
with his pocketknife like a hunter,
his law and mind untouchable,
certain of the correction necessary.
Back inside, he rams the bathroom door,
the hook popping. He yanks open
the shower curtain, revealing the boy
who can't tell what weapon of choice
the intruder holds, dark and blurry.

I want to get in between the blinded child
and the screwup who's trying
to be his father, to take the hits.
The man's shouting gibberish, the kid's
trying to protect his dick, the switch
landing on his arms, chest, thighs,
stomach, shoulders, hard enough to sting
but bruise minimally. The man's got enough control
not to hit his face, his hands, anywhere
those welts can be seen. The way the pain settling
into softer flesh is the man's way of saying
this boy's spoiled life isn't so bad.
He could've gotten the axe.

GIRL BARN

Alphabet Love

My mother names Zany and Escher after their psychedelic,
black-and-white hides. The shaggy cows she calls Ozzy
and Yoko. Dumb momma Daffy begets Dipstick.

Like a librarian she collects one of every letter: Alice and Gertrude,
Mushroom and Kesey, Hester and Ursula in a barn row
across from Inky, Queen, Fantasia, Jinx, Pandora, and Beauty,

rivals of the three sisters
Solar, Luna, and Umbra, who in turn
butt heads with Raggedy, Viola, and Never-Never.

Turning Against

Their noses black detectors
of vibration, cows examine every inch of wire.
There they go, over and through, the fence
dragged, ticking feeble underfoot.
I don't want to chase them back inside,
into the tangle of steel and rubber
tubes, the milkers attaching like spiders.
In the free minutes before my family
finds them, they gorge on soft cobs
and sweet husks, alfalfa fresh
from the root, and wander toward the lake.
When my parents find out, I have to join them
with dirt clods and rocks,
scare our bad girls back home.

Sapphic Pastoral

In need of no bull, the girls
are riding the one in heat,
her clear honey quickening.
One mounts her, she scoots, another
sneaks behind, climbs up again.

In the barn, my mother slips her hand
into the plastic glove, tugs the tips
of her fingers into place, unwraps
this odd condom up
to her aching shoulder.

Never Give a Cow Your Name

the way my little sister did. Theresa seemed sweet and innocent
but grew so much faster than a girl, until the calf it once was
towered over her. The gangly heifer
still wanted to cuddle and play, knocked her down,
licked her like a block of salt until my sister couldn't
control her fear anymore, announced how much

she hated Theresa. When she entered the pasture,
the heifer sniffed her out, its head lowered
like a mean girl, charged to let that child know
who was boss. In tears, my sister cowered
in front of the beast my mother and I hit and chased,
the monster she hadn't meant to invent.

VISITING MY OTHER MOTHER

For years the hope ripens.
My aunt, a nurse, asks about the odd marks
on my back and the scars too. She notices
anything off or wrong,
asks why, at my age,
I don't have a girlfriend. By my curt answer
and her silence, she senses
I'm somehow lying. Knowing my father
better than anyone, she can part
the curtain of my pimply body
and maybe, I worry, really see
my father happening to my face
and brain. Or how I double
as the force field
containing him for everyone. If she cared less,
it would hurt less.
Returning over time, I start to believe
if I strike the perfect balance between brother and cousin, if I play
by every rule, one day she will say
I can't bear for you to go back there.

MY MOTHER WITH DOZENS OF GAY SONS

In the runaway story where my mother keeps me,
never to return home, we end up in Portland
        instead of the farm. She cuts all family ties.

Under the tag of Magdalene, she graffitis
murals of gangs of priests fucking boy-Jesus,
        Jesus growing wondrous breasts

illuminating believers, Jesus naked with a boner
on a horse, a halo around the asshole
        of bottom-Jesus, begging on all fours.

We're vandals wanted by the church.
The first time I borrow her tag to draw Christ
        kissing a disciple with tongue, she knows.

Her only kid, I come out when I'm ten,
spend my teen years falling in love with gay boys
        who get kicked out of their homes.

They move into my room, sleep
in my bed, new ones all the time,
        sometimes two

at a time. Pushing condoms, my mother knows
full well what's going on, glad
        boys can't get pregnant.

Welcome even after
we break up, all her sons visit
        once a year for gay Christmas.

We discover new sex toys underneath
the tree decorated with hand-painted cock
        ornaments of all sizes and colors,

everyone eventually getting old enough
that she will drop into each pink stocking
        one organic, hand-rolled joint.

    When we smoke it, we dream of getting tagged
in nocturnal technicolor, cocks jumping into coats,
        assholes iridescent with wishes.

FOR BOYS WHO TEACH THEMSELVES TO USE
THEIR MOTHERS' MAKEUP ON BRUISES

First, you consider how well the flesh tone will conceal you
from casual eyes, then the prying kind.

You've learned pretty girls shouldn't be bruised,
but you're a boy, quietly trained in your family's ploys.

You get good enough grades and speak with smiles
and charm your teachers into looking away.

Throughout the day, you check your camouflage,
reapply in toilet stalls. You buy more

at the drug store, and if your pockets are ever searched,
you can say the makeup belongs to your beards.

Your glamers make everyone else see
those handsome sweet talkers, not the toughs

who know how to take being humiliated, slugged.
You do and you don't want anyone to notice

how rocklike you really are, how proudly
you defy your beaters, how you make them work for it.

You fear what will happen when your foundation
fails, and a friend or stranger who's not a fool

asks what someone has been doing to you and who
they are. That's what you worry will break you.

A FEW WORDS ABOUT MY LAZINESS

One morning while I slept, my stepdad hit me with a steel pipe,
                    the one he kept in the barn. He clubbed me again
          the way he would strike a cow that lay too long,
                              wouldn't stand to be milked. Cursing him,
               I hurried to sit up, took it again in the ribs
                    like a bad girl, climbed out of bed in my underwear,
          my little sack of an udder bouncing.
                              Landing next to him, I was ready to do
          what very little a twelve-year-old closeted boy could do
                    with fists and teeth, whatever hopeless stand could be taken
                              against a man three times his size.
I wished for a cow's girth and weight, her horns and hooves.
                    Satisfied now, all he wanted to say
          were a few words about my laziness. I understood
                    he was testing my limits, learning
     how much of a beating I could take,
                    estimating how much more,
               with the proper training, I might bear.

AN EVENING WITH A SLEEPWALKER IN THE ROOM

No one knows how long I stood
over my mother's sleeping husband,
a folded-up metal chair in my hands
    raised and ready.

They woke up together saying,
drop it, put it down, put it back
over and over to the dumb, white
    dog of my face.

VI.

MY LIFE AS CREEP BOY

In the childhood fable where I struggle to read
and write like a normal kid but can't,

I like to break a frog's legs, slice
its white belly, hang it

on the barb of a fence until its heart stops.
I huff gas, start fires, stare numb at hot dads,

but I'm a talker. I get in your head.
Barely seventeen, I find my first

lonely, giving daddy
to suck, spit out like old candy.

I flunk out of school but graduate
to the web. I'll trick you out of your clothes,

beat you when you don't bend over,
and if you dare tell, I'll deny everything.

CRIMINAL WISHES

For my father to kidnap me
from my bedroom, his hand over my mouth
though I'd go willing to his car
full of crumpled cans
of Old Milwaukee
and buckle up.

To be in his care,
dye my hair,
change my name,
age like a runaway,
and make out with older boys
in secret, sweet talk
their billfolds open
to steal their IDs.

To shoplift smokes for him
in the armpit of my jean jacket,
roll his road-trip joints, steer
when he can't see the center line.

To break into cars
in underground lots
as I look for pain pills
like precious stones.

To help him hustle
a new copper-haired girl
into falling in love, having a baby
she gets to keep long after
we pour her waitressing tips
into a cheap plastic bag
like Halloween candy
and hit the open road.

MY FATHER, REBORN AS A HEALER

He's born again in the asylum where Jesus
and Buddha heal him. Their monk now, he visits our house
        for the first time with a mixed-up tract

    he wrote on the heart, beating large as a church,
encircled by people holding hands, their palms
        ready to be nailed to the sky on judgment

    day but swelling with dharma love anyway.
Saying he's been delivered from bondages of evil,
        he's never met real gays, he's unable to speak

    of my harmless husband in the first person,
and he's not going to stop obsessing about abominations
        who walk the unsuspecting earth

    in shiny, red shoes. He proclaims, with the right petal,
he can heal anyone. Besides antipsychotics, his only drugs
        are three daily doses of the Lord.

    He never knew what to do with a son, still doesn't.
To ease him, I testify with lies. Yes, I believe
        in the story of the inmate with one blind eye,

    how my father waved a white rose
under the man's nose. I'm certain, like a thunderclap,
        the scent flashed, bringing back the light.

LIVES MY MOTHER LIVES DOING CHORES

Lifting rocks, my mother, the private detective,
catches the killer. It's the deputy. He's got another
teenage girl. When he flashes his badge
like a pardon, she shoots his hand
and both measly kneecaps.

Shoveling gutters, my mother, the first female
Major League Baseball player, hits a home run
into the stands. Her ball breaks the president's nose,
and he cries like a little girl on camera.
Refusing to apologize, she riles the country.

Trying to sleep between milkings, my mother,
the radical, punches a priest in the face
outside an abortion clinic. She graffitis
right-wing churches like boxcars
and crashes their services with signs
condemning God. She goes to jail happy.

OUTSIDE IN THE DARK

The black cow fits
like a puzzle piece
into the rest of the hill.

Hungry bug songs
playing from every leaf
draw me in.

A car goes down
the snaking gravel road,
a light being swallowed.

AFTER THE SLEEPWALKERS MAKE THEIR ROUNDS

We wake up to masses of newspapers
glued like windows to living room walls,
tables set proper, marbles and dry rice

waiting in breakfast bowls, fresh cat litter
coating welcome mats, hoses left running
in wheelbarrows filled with guppies, bras

tied to limbs, underwear nested in branches,
our hopeless pranksters embarrassed
by all they don't know they do, by the days

that pass before anyone finds the tools
missing, the chest tossed like trash, or the dead
birds stuffed into socks, buried in the whites.

TOWN COWS

Like oversized rabbits, they jump
their fences for the streets, stopping traffic
with their one message. They sack
curb gardens, munch tulips
to nubs. Chased, they bolt
like deer. Calm, they let
total strangers stroke their ears.
Raising their tails like spigots,
they shit on everyone's sidewalks.
At night it's just the same. We find them
lurking in backyards, gulping irises, their heads
in the raised beds like troughs, their tails
swinging, starting a rumpus.

VII.

THE SLEEPWALKER, TO HIS HUSBAND

I hope you won't find me
wandering naked

out the front door,
carrying underwear

like a lunch bag
in my hand,

but if you do, please
get shoes and clothes,

get them on me.
Follow me, wherever

I go—the streets, the cars,
and shady bars.

Order me
a drink, tell me

you love me. Take
my hand, don't

turn me around.
Walk this wanderer,

whomever he is,
back into his eyes.

EIGHT DREAMS ON THE RUN WITH MY FATHER

Small as a doll, I crawl inside him when he sleeps.
Worried about where I've gone, all day he searches for me.

~

From his car trunk he unpacks a box of butterfly wings,
thoraxes gone. I throw them until two lift off, alive again.

~

We move from town to town, squat in empty apartments.
Meals from tin cans and candles so the landlords won't know.

~

Some mornings all I do is erase my face from milk cartons,
replace it with the dead boy of the day.

~

Windows rolled up, doors locked, we drive into the lake.
Breaths held, water rising, he turns into an eel, teaches me.

~

Days later, on shore, the hills are yelling at the wind.
I'm sandy and wet. He's singing, taking the sky's side.

~

Sudden headlights illuminate our scars, sunken
underneath skin. Visible only in the flash, we're seen.

~

At last, I notice I'm driving. Right now, he's the boy,
the one who crawled out of my belly, buckled up.

NOW THAT MY FATHER HAS FOUND ME

He knocks on my front door for the first time,
but I can't get up from bed or open my eyes.
My hand twitches, wanting to answer.

Once inside, it's darker than the rest
of the dark, but he hasn't taken a step.
He's pulling my house

closer, my pillow too, his smoke
in my paralyzed ear, two fingers
like tweezers prying an eyelid.

WANDERER WITH BLACK HOLE

Suppose, in an accident of time travel,
the transmitter stuffs me into the body
of a farm kid from 1950, our lives

parallel in like-isolation. The son
of another rough father, he sleepwalks
the nowheres of snowdrifts and ditches.

In his brain, I no longer need to sleep.
At night, with too much time
to think, I float down his joints,

lift fingers, remember legs.
The more I move his teenage body,
the more he dreams my memories,

Morse code from a similar self.
Each time he writes down a story, I pull him
like light into the curve of our collision.

ON THE THIRTIETH ANNIVERSARY OF MY
RESURRECTION

Soon will arrive my lonely birthday,
the day my stepdad choked Mike, the name

I no longer use, the boy who suffocated
into unknowable darkness. After months there,

a minute in clock time, my body took a breath.
For hours after I returned, doors and walls dissolved

at the pressure of my touch. For a moment
I would feel the nothingness where I had floated,

that nowhere underneath and within
the world, every flower and stone

a vibration achieving primitive and false solidity.
Too much for fifteen,

this understanding of emptiness the mystic seeks—
I never wanted it. But its infliction

has tuned my senses toward that nothing,
normed alone and over time through force of will.

I needed to believe
the boy had survived a kind of murder,

come back intact. My necessary delusion.
With handprints entangling my throat,

I joined the family for supper, a civil, silent meal
disguising the wake.

BARN RADIO

The cows stand entranced in their stalls.
Through cheap speakers splattered
brown, Beethoven blares.
With black spots like receivers, their bodies
absorb the sound. All four chambers
of their stomachs reverberate.

The sounds circulate all day.
In the evening, they get pop radio.
They listen to country songs about babies who don't
come back, good lovin', and bad women.
Each night they go to sleep with our human gibberish
like background noise to their dreams, our bodiless
voices muttering all night.

THE GHOST STORY THEY TELL ABOUT YOU

Dear Father, did you know the summer you spent in the hospital
in St. Peter for the dangerous and mentally ill,

I was in town too? I was falling in love with a boy
at summer camp, thinking about you in a straitjacket,

strapped down for shock therapy, drugged up
and playing cards with other lunatics, not that I knew

anything about your diagnosis or days. I only knew I blew
our best chance to meet. You couldn't leave.

I could've brought my secret boyfriend, a deck of cards,
dealt a game of hearts for three. I could've let you win.

Would you have told me what it felt like to nail your house
shut, window and door, your wife and daughter

asleep inside, how quiet you kept your hammer?
And after you started the fire, how you stuck around

to watch the show or split to smoke or pop something
in celebration? I would've listened because I wanted

to know who you were really burning, how
happy or terrible you felt when your wife wrenched

open a window, the two of them scared out of their minds.
I wanted to know what black magic charms you used

on my mother, then my aunt, while you called
our house saying *I know where you live, bitch,*

and I'm gonna getcha. For years I mouthed your threat
like the alphabet, those secondhand words.

How many teenage girlfriends did you get pregnant
in your forty-eight years, how many other kids still out there?

And why did women keep falling for you? There are no answers
about the night you and your brother, playing with a gun,

shot and killed your little sister. Did you pull the trigger? Did you
blame him? My mother swears it; my aunt defends you.

About your brother: I want to know if your lie could've forced you
to your feet during the eulogy after his suicide to cry out

You don't know shit about pain to the priest. The day you chased
your mother with a knife out of her house, then your father

down the alley with a gun shooting wildly, I knew
I'd never know the truth about you. I was thirteen,

worried I might start hearing gravestones speak,
wake up one morning covered in my family's blood.

ACKNOWLEDGMENTS

Variations of these poems appeared in the following publications:

Assaracus: "Criminal Wishes," "The Cousin Act," "An Evening with a Sleepwalker in the Room," "The Ghost Story They Tell about You," and "Scratched-Out Name"

Birmingham Poetry Review: "Town Cows"

Cherry Tree: "On the Thirtieth Anniversary of My Resurrection," "Sex with Jesus," "The Likely Darkness," and "To the Brightness"

Cimarron Review: "A Few Words about My Laziness" and "My Mother as a Pregnant Teenage Runaway"

The Cincinnati Review: "The Sleepwalker, to His Husband"

Crab Creek Review: "Granary Zen" and "Turning Against" (excerpted from "Girl Barn")

Crab Orchard Review: "For Boys Who Teach Themselves to Use Their Mothers' Makeup on Bruises" (as "To the Boys Who Teach Themselves to Use Their Mothers' Makeup on Bruises")

Cream City Review: "The Antigay Retelling of My Life" and "My Mother with Dozens of Gay Sons"

Fiddleblack: "The Ghost Story They Tell about Me," "My Life as Creep Boy," "Now That My Father Has Found Me," "To the Specter," and "Wanderer with Black Hole"

The Good Men Project: "Anticipation of the Knife"

Great River Review: "Barn Radio"

The Journal: "The Queer as Electron"

The Main Street Rag: "My Father, Reborn as a Healer" (as "My Father, a True Believer")

Midwestern Gothic: "Sapphic Pastoral" (excerpted from "Girl Barn")

Mudfish: "Dick" and "In the Dream Mistaken for a Memory"

the museum of americana: "Outside in the Dark" and "Summer Intruder"

Pangyrus: "Switch or Axe"

Pittsburgh Poetry Review: "Visiting My Other Mother"

Prairie Schooner: "Lives My Mother Lives Doing Chores"

Southern Poetry Review: "Sleepwalks"

Tinderbox Poetry Journal: "Fence Catching Heart" and "Pastoral, Underfoot" (as "Pastoral with Boot")

"Sleepwalks" also appeared in a chapbook of the same title, published by Red Dragonfly Press in 2012.

Michael Walsh received his BA in English (Writing) from Knox College and his MFA in Creative and Professional Writing from the University of Minnesota, Twin Cities. His poetry books include *The Dirt Riddles* (University of Arkansas Press) as well as two chapbooks, *Adam Walking the Garden* and *Sleepwalks*, both published by Red Dragonfly Press. Along with James Crews, he is the co-editor of *Queer Nature*, a poetry anthology forthcoming from Autumn House Press. His poems and stories have appeared in journals such as *Alaska Quarterly Review, Birmingham Poetry Review, The Chattahoochee Review, Cherry Tree, Cimarron Review, Crab Orchard Review, Great River Review, The Journal, North Dakota Quarterly, Prairie Schooner, South Dakota Review,* and *Southern Poetry Review*. His poems have also been adapted as librettos by the composer Marcos Balter. He lives in Minneapolis and works as a curriculum administrator at the University of Minnesota and as an independent scholar and creative writing instructor.

NEW AND FORTHCOMING RELEASES

No One Leaves the World Unhurt by John Foy ♦ Winner of the 2020
Donald Justice Poetry Prize, selected by J. Allyn Rosser

Lucky Wreck: Anniversary Edition by Ada Limón

In the Antarctic Circle by Dennis James Sweeney ♦ Winner of the 2020
Autumn House Rising Writer Prize, selected by Yona Harvey

Creep Love by Michael Walsh

The Dream Women Called by Lori Wilson

"American" Home by Sean Cho A. ♦ Winner of the 2020
Autumn House Chapbook Prize, selected by Danusha Laméris

Under the Broom Tree by Natalie Homer

Molly by Kevin Honold ♦ Winner of the 2020 Autumn House
Fiction Prize, selected by Dan Chaon

The Animal Indoors by Carly Inghram ♦ Winner of the 2020 CAAPP
Book Prize, selected by Terrance Hayes

speculation, n. by Shayla Lawz ♦ Winner of the 2020 Autumn House
Poetry Prize, selected by Ilya Kaminsky

All Who Belong May Enter by Nicholas Ward ♦ Winner of the 2020 Autumn
House Nonfiction Prize, selected by Jaquira Díaz

For our full catalog please visit: http://www.autumnhouse.org